KILL THE
ROCK STAR

Worship's Heart Unveiled

ISBN 978-1-621660-64-4

Published by XP Publishing
A department of XP Ministries

P.O. Box 1017
Maricopa, Arizona 85139
www.XPPublishing.com

KILL THE ROCK STAR

Worship's Heart Unveiled

BY SANDY LOCKHART

Here's what others are saying about

Kill the Rock Star...

I have known Sandy Lockhart for many years and have seen her consistently walk in humility and integrity before God as she grew in her anointing, gifting, and public presence. She is truly a woman whose heart can be trusted, and I fully see why God chose her to pen this prophetic appeal.

I love this book, and its important message in this critical hour will raise the bar in a day where celebrity fascination and idolatry is becoming increasingly prevalent. There is ONE to be exalted above all else, and Sandy KNOWS Him well. She will lead you to be fascinated in Him alone.

Although it is written primarily for worship leaders, it is a book that every believer should read. Receive the invitation that is clearly given in *Kill the Rockstar*, live the invitation, and then GO and share it with others. Yes, share it with many others.

PATRICIA KING

Founder, XPministries, AZ. & XPmedia, INC.
XPministries.com
XPmedia.com

In *Kill the Rock Star*, Sandy brings clear definition to the role of the worship leader, which is to lead people into an encounter with the presence of God. But at different times, God wants to reveal different aspects of who He is: our Father, Healer, Bridegroom, Captain of the Lord's army, etc. There are also times when the Lord desires to sing over us and tell us how He sees us as His beloved children, friends, beloved bride, and more.

For this to happen, the worship leader must be able to LISTEN and then lead. Sounds simple enough; yet if the worship leader is motivated by their need for recognition, affirmation, and the approval of men, their mixed motives cloud their lens and wrong motives contaminate their filters. If the worship leader cannot see and hear the Lord clearly, they cannot follow Him or lead others into a place to experience Him.

Sandy takes us on her journey and graciously illustrates how the Holy Spirit purifies and refines our motives to become the TRUE WORSHIPPERS our Father seeks. She brilliantly equips us with the understanding of how a worship leader must learn to live in between the tension of pastoral concern for the people and the prophetic concern of where and how the Holy Spirit is leading. Sandy will help you to place your ear on the Lord's heart, and your finger on the pulse of the people you lead.

BRUCE FRIESEN

Visionary Leader, Lion of Judah Ministries, Victoria, BC
lionofjudah.ca

The first time I met Sandy was at a conference where I was a speaker, and I was so blessed when this mighty General in God's army stood up to lead worship! From the first note sung, the authority Sandy walks in was evident; she entered into the rivers of the Spirit and led out into the deep place of prophetic declarations and devotion that cleared the way for the glory of God. His presence was tangible; the atmosphere was electric, and the chains were broken as worship opened the heavens for His glory to invade.

Rising up is a bridal company of worship leaders whose lives are fully His and whose hearts are united with the sounds and the agenda of heaven. Sandy has been a disciple taught of the Lord, and her honesty, insight, and depth will ignite a passion to let go of the surface, and delve into the deep places of His heart.

I highly recommend this book to worshippers, especially those chosen to lead others into His glorious presence through the prophetic terrain of the undiscovered land of His Spirit, where there is always more of His amazing love to experience. Worshippers arise!

Cathryn Nash

Pastor, Frontline Ministries, Sylvan Lake, AB
frontlineministries-int.com

I loved it! So raw, so real! Having had the privilege of walking closely with Sandy for many years and counting her as a dear friend, I can honestly say that I have seen the heart of this book lived out and tested in her life. Her love for the Lord and surrender to Him in worship has inspired many, helping them shift their mindsets in worship. This is a precious handbook for all who have been called to release worship!

Tabitha LeMaire

Mont-Saint-Hilaire, Quebec, Canada
tabithasings.com

If anyone has the authority to write a book with this title it is Sandy Lockhart. *Kill the Rock Star* is insightful, practical, and heavenly minded in all the right ways. Not only do I recommend it for worship leaders but for anyone who is called to public ministry. Thank you for keeping it real, Sandy. Awesome.

Faytene Grasseschi

Best Selling Author
Director of TheCRY Movement & MY Canada

Sandy Lockhart is one of our favorite worship leaders. She has a God-given ability to move in the Spirit and follow the winds of God in praise and worship. This book is a great tool for all those leading worship, desiring to lead worship, and for all those who love to spend time in His presence.

Because she has allowed God to do such a thorough sifting in her life, Sandy knows how to move herself out of the way and allow God to move in. We highly recommend this book.

Charlie & Shirley Robinson

Canadian Revivalists

Dedicated to

the worshipping Levites…

and all who long to live in the courts of the Lord.

CONTENTS

Foreword   13

1.   Look Up   17

2.   Imagine   25

3.   Lower Still   37

4.   Saturated Sound   47

5.   Hidden   55

6.   The Deep   65

7.   Industry   73

8.   The Journey   81

FOREWORD

BY

JANET ANGELA MILLS

Imagine the most beautiful, lush, and fruitful paradise. It is the most perfect climate and heavenly atmosphere. In this place there is divine health and wholeness. There is pure joy and God's richest blessings are everywhere in sight. Now remember that Adam and Eve were created and lived in that realm. They lived in direct contact with Father God, and they communed with Him constantly. God's original intention was to live with man in a place of abundant blessing. A close intimate connection with the Creator of Heaven and earth...

Praise and worship are intended to be the communication between God and us. Praise and worship are not just things we do, but they are who we are. They are tools to usher in the very glory of God! There is restoration made available through Christ for everyone who believes in His saving power. His desire is that we encounter Him and His glory, as He has always intended, for us to be one with Him.

Our praise changes the atmosphere around us! God's desire is for us to be those who would worship in spirit and truth! "But the hour cometh, and now is, when the true worshippers shall worship the Father in spirit and in truth; for the Father seeketh such to worship him. God is a Spirit: and they that worship him must worship him in spirit and truth" (John 4: 23-24).

I can sincerely say that Sandy is one of those that God desires… a true worshipper! Sandy has become a dear and close friend, and she reflects the Lord's glory and love! She is one of the most loving and compassionate people I know. She walks in true humility, and her worship comes from a deep intimacy with our Savior! She knows Him, and He knows her!

Through these pages, Sandy opens up her heart and takes you on her beautiful journey... This book will inspire and challenge you to examine your heart! It will expose the motives of your heart and bring great freedom; this book will show you how to *let go* and *let God*!

God has blessed each one of us with a voice to release His glory and to release His sounds. Every worship leader and musician should read this with an open heart to receive an impartation from the Lord. There are practical activations shared in this book, which will propel you toward a more intimate relationship with Christ.

God has destined you for greatness, and He wants to reveal just how great He is inside of you!

In His Great Love,
Janet Angela Mills

New Wine International Ministries
NewWineInternational.org

ONE

LOOK UP

Music is one of the most valuable gifts given to us. In my life, music has been a key that unlocks and exposes a secret place within my being that nothing else created can access. Music is a language my heart understands. I have seen music cross every human boundary – age, gender, ethnicity, language, culture, and socio-economic status – to bring a crowd of people together in focus.

I have observed and felt music change the atmosphere of a room, based on the songs' lyrical content and musical style. For example, when a fiddle player begins a jig, people begin to dance with enthusiasm. When a drummer begins a strong beat, your body begins to respond by clapping or tapping your foot. I have also been in situations where a musician begins to play a song that holds very personal, heartfelt content, and many in the room begin to identify with the emotion – positive or negative – being released. As the corporate gathering of people begin to identify with the emotion, the atmosphere shifts. You can often feel it. Something has changed, and people respond whether they understand why or not.

AN AMAZING GIFT

I believe that when music is played in an attitude and heart posture of worship, it is not only one of our greatest gifts, but also one of our greatest weapons in the spirit realm. When we learn to use this weapon effectively, we will begin to manifest who we really are: carriers of God's presence, bringing the Kingdom of Heaven to earth through song!

When I think about worship, and when I think about the power of worship, I am overwhelmed with the goodness of God and how great He is. What a plan He has for us! It is His plan that man be fully alive, and live to worship Him.

He has given us the gifts of music and worship to bring us closer to His heart and to allow us to know Him more intimately. He calls us to journey with Him as He speaks to us and changes us at a heart level through music. And then He allows us to respond in thanksgiving by worshipping Him and lifting His name here on the earth!

We are all called to different positions within the Kingdom of God. One of my primary functions in the body is to lead worship through prophetic and intercessory song. I know this is who I am and what I am called to. There are many facets involved in the journey of discovering your position in the Kingdom. For me, the most important facet has always been, and will always be, spending time with Jesus in worship, reading His word, and listening to His heart. I become fully awake and fully alive in His presence, and I learn who I am through those times.

CARRIERS OF GLORY

My journey began at the age of eight when I started leading worship. I had a gift, a calling, and a destiny, just as you do. I was marked with authority, and I was intended for glory, just as you are. While you and I were still being formed, God's DNA was being woven into us so we would be His glory. We would have the potential to carry the same glory that Jesus carried when He walked the earth. We have spiritual gifts that we can open, play with, use, and enjoy. We are given a choice: We can use our gifts for ourselves – our expression, glory, and fame for worldly gain – or we can consecrate ourselves and use our gifts for Him – His heart's expression, His glory, and fame.

> Since, then, you have been raised with Christ, set your hearts on things above, where Christ is, seated at the right hand of God. Set your minds on things above, not on earthly things. For you died, and your life is now hidden with Christ in God.
>
> —Colossians 3:1-3

SEE ONLY JESUS

Have you ever been in a crowded city and observed someone looking up? What if that person begins to point up to the sky and ask people walking by, "Do you see that? What is it?" Many will begin to stop and lift their eyes to search out whatever is so captivating. Some won't bother, as the pressures of time push them past the opportunity. Others may be fearful of what might be in the skies so they won't dare take their focus off the ground. Some will be indifferent, while others will be sure they already know what is up there, and they will not bother to look again. And, finally, there are those who won't even listen to the invitation.

I believe, as leaders of worship, our job is to look up. We are commissioned to be those in the crowd who stand, point to the sky, and draw others to look at what we see. We cause them to set their minds on things above. We inspire worship in others by worshipping with all that we have. We come boldly before the throne of grace and worship Him face to face, because we are seated with Him in heavenly places.

We are beckoned to take our focus off of ourselves and fix our eyes on the King, and we call others to do the same. We are designated to live a consecrated, righteous life, and we are called as priests to minister before the Lord.

John Wesley was once asked, "Why do people come to watch you minister?" He replied, "I set myself on fire and people come to watch me burn." We need to burn with longing and desire for the One whom our hearts love; then our love becomes attractive to the spirit of God and to those around us.

On my journey, I have not always chosen what is right. I have stumbled, messed up, hurt others, sought recognition, found identity in my gifting, and walked in pride and false humility. I have engaged with a dangerous spirit of entitlement that would suggest I deserve accolades and praise because of my hard work and the wonderful music I created.

The questions I've asked myself are: How do I kill the inner rock star – the place of ego and pride that lives a self-centered, self-gratifying, self-indulgent life-style – and learn to consecrate every part of my life to God? How do I lead worship with pure motives? How can I walk in righteousness and purity in the role for which I am created? What does it really mean to be a worship leader?

> Let us fix our eyes on Jesus, the author and perfector of our faith, who for the joy set before him endured the cross, scorning its shame, and sat down at the right hand of the throne of God.
>
> —Hebrews 12:2

THE COST

Being a worship leader is no small assignment; it is not something we can look at lightly. One of the first things we must consider is our motivation. Why do I seek the spotlight of the stage? Is it because I am a Christian and a musician, or is it because I can't do anything but worship, and I am ruined for anything else but to exalt the name of the Lord?

You may be marked as a worship leader if you are compelled to lead others into a posture of worship; you yearn to hear the corporate sound of worship rise as incense to Jesus, and you long to bring honor to our King through song.

The cost must be carefully weighed before the Lord, because the price is everything you are and everything you ever will be. Life as a worshipper is like precious metal, which must be refined in fire to remove impurities. Our call is to be purified in the Holy Spirit's fire, submitted to His authority, and to allow Him to search our hearts daily (see Zechariah 13:9).

What a joy to be whom God has called and created us to be! It is a privilege to play our part as worship leaders in the body of Christ. Our mandate is to magnify Jesus: we sing straight to Him, pour our love on Him, and look into the face of the One our heart adores.

We must go low to show Jesus high and lifted up. When He is our motivation and we move in Him, those around us will begin to look up. Will you be the one?

Now to him who is able to do immeasurably more than all we ask or imagine, according to his power that is at work within us.

—Ephesians 3:20

IMAGINE

Imagine with me for a moment... Your anticipation
for an upcoming worship set has been growing for
months, and your preparations have been day and
night. You and your team have received word that there
will be a royal visitation during the service. You will be
playing for the King. He will be visiting your church,
and healings and miracles are on His agenda. Every
waking moment you have focused on how to prepare
for this service. Even as you sleep, pictures of this coming encounter find their way into your dreams.

Now, imagine leading worship from this posture of anticipation, knowing the King is already here and, in fact, lives in us! How the environments of our churches, families, cities, culture, and nations would change when those on our worship teams, independently, spend deliberate time in daily prayer, seeking the Lord to ask what *He* wants to do.

Imagine your heart bursting, full of God's Spirit, and your anticipation soaring because you believe the Bible when it says that *anything* is possible. What happens when we know that the Spirit of God lives in us and that God is for us?

> The spirit of God, who raised Jesus from the dead, lives in you ... What shall we say about such wonderful things as these? If God is for us, who can ever be against us?
>
> —Romans 8:11a, 31, NLT

We can be confident that we are His glory and when we open our mouth, He fills it! Let us infuse our worship leading with the spirit of faith that will move mountains.

I like to be still before I lead a set. I take a moment to let that spirit of faith rise on the inside of me, and I pray to align myself with whatever the Lord desires to do. While I do not follow a formula, there *are* some actions that I often find myself doing: I speak truth over myself and the congregation. I speak out and agree with those around me that today is the day for heaven to be released on earth. I say the Lord's Prayer and let my faith be stirred. I do what I need to do to posture my spirit in anticipation and faith, and then I lead the worship. I speak scriptures that stir my heart and align with a theme or concept that is in place. (For example, if I'm leading at a conference with a love theme, I focus on love.)

ATMOSPHERE SHIFTERS

I shift my own atmosphere so that I can shift the corporate atmosphere. Within my spirit, I prophetically hold what the Lord desires to be released in worship. I begin to release it from the inside out, praying and interceding over the people as I lead them in worship. Maybe this is what Paul was talking about when he said to pray without ceasing (1 Thessalonians 5:17). God always gives opportunity to prophetically step into what He has placed inside me for that venue, and then it is up to me to be bold and release it!

Sometimes the Lord's theme comes to my heart through a color, picture, word, scripture, or dream, etc. For example, if I see the color green in my spirit as I pray and prepare – or even after I have begun worship – and I know that green often represents new life, I begin to carry the theme of new life in my heart. I pray over the people that new life will begin to spring up where death came in. I pray that new dreams and visions, and new releases of glory will be found in the house where I am ministering. I hold these things in my heart as I worship, waiting with *great* anticipation for the moment when I can begin to prophetically minister to the people on this topic. I wait, knowing that the second I can begin to release the word of the Lord, great and mighty things are going to happen!

When we anticipate the Kingdom of Heaven will be released in worship, it will absolutely shift the atmosphere. When I lay hold of a truth in Scripture, not only do I come alive, but life also flows from me to those I lead.

Scripture clearly states that the same spirit (the same authority) that raised Jesus from His grave is on the inside of us. God is *for* us – He wants the best for us! He longs for us to see ourselves the way He sees us. God's perspective is what we can be. He sees us as atmosphere shifters! We are those who know our authority because of who Christ is in us. In our spirit and with our mouth we can take control of situations to bring them into alignment with heaven. We are those who can speak to the winds and the waves, "Peace be still."

We are those who know we are His home... a tabernacle for His glory... pure. We hold the potential to walk in the same power and authority that Christ did, because we are His glory, and His glory is in us. We can do the things He did, and He gets the glory!

When we receive this revelation of living our lives for *His* glory and for *His* fame, we are *free*. We can get off center stage and allow Him to take over. When we understand this truth, not just for ourselves but for those we lead, our hearts begin to beat with compassion and love for the body of Christ. God is love; therefore, He is attracted to an atmosphere of love.

LISTEN, *THEN* LEAD

As I lead worship, I often look to see where the Spirit of God is moving, whom He is moving on, and what the responses are to His Spirit. Sometimes I observe tears or exuberance, and other times there seems to be reflection. I ask the Lord where to go and follow *His* leading. I may feel prompted to do a specific song, repeat a line from a song we are singing, or maybe just play something instrumental. It totally depends on what the Spirit says in that moment. It is called *context*. Listen, and *then* lead. When you cooperate with the Spirit, this becomes natural. It is often described as flowing in a river, and that really is what it feels like.

You never completely know where the current will take you, but when you have surrendered control, you flow in the safety of the Ultimate Worship Leader.

THE INNER DIVA

Like many, there are tensions that I live in: I cry out for the glory of God to come and dwell, be made manifest, and consume me. But I also know that I am made in the image of Christ, and His glory lives *within* me. I long to see God's glory with my eyes: to walk up the mountain, as Moses did, and boldly step into the cloud of God's presence. I long to physically and spiritually shine because I have been so close to the King that He is reflected in me. I want to see the world changed because of Him, and I know the potential is inside of me to do everything that Jesus did. So, what stops me from manifesting this life?

I understand that I have the same power that raised Christ from the dead on the inside of me, and yet, I put *my* needs and *my* desires first. That is the diva part of me – my inner rock star. My falsely humble personality says that it is all about Jesus; I am for the King. However, my actions often show that, if I had to make the choice, I would rather not be inconvenienced by the needs around me. I want what I want, when I want it.

TRANSFORMED IN WORSHIP

So how do we get the knowledge from our head to our heart? How do we put God first? One key is to surround ourselves with friends who breathe life into our "calls" and giftings, because they summon them forth. Be with those who encourage you and whom you can encourage. Also, simply choose, day-by-day and minute-by-minute, to be a house for His glory.

Most importantly, we must experience God. Tremendous transformation takes place as we worship Him. He brings us into encounters with Him where He waters and encourages our spirit and activates our gifts and call. As we give the Lord worship, He showers back upon our hearts. The more we step into a place of worshipping in spirit and truth, the more we are brought to life. God's presence keeps our heart and mind focused on things above, not on things of the earth.

We are called as individuals and as a corporate bride to be a resting place for God's glory – a tabernacle. We have a responsibility to come before the Lord, bow low, and spend our lives on Him. The ultimate life is one that is lived for Him, wholly surrendered – He consumes our every move, action, and thought.

Sound ideal? It is. Can we achieve it? Absolutely. Ask! Ask to be a resting place for His glory, to be consecrated by Him and for Him. Ask the Lord to be your source, motivation, and strength. If we make Him our dwelling place, He will come and find a home.

A ROYAL PRIESTHOOD

What if we live as we were created to live: as a royal priesthood and a holy nation? What if we live as those who respond to His voice with faith instead of questions and doubt: "Did He speak? Did I actually hear what I thought I heard?"

Test the word the Lord gives you, but do not live in a place of doubt when He speaks. When the Lord speaks, say *yes*! When you are leading and feel to go in a certain direction, go! When you are faithful with little, He will trust you with much.

As a royal priesthood, we are set apart for His glory. God sees us as a Holy Nation. He sees us differently than we view ourselves. When we see through His eyes our lives will change as we begin to live out who we *really* are. When we see with His eyes, it sets us free to live unselfishly and give everything to Him.

MARKED

As a worshipper, you are marked with holiness. Holiness is not something we can take lightly. There are many Biblical examples of those who took holiness lightly and paid the ultimate price with their lives. Consecration is not something we want to mess around with or a word to throw around loosely. Some of us are marked to carry the Lord's presence in the same way the Levites did. We are marked, chosen, and trusted by the Lord to be faithful and lead the people into His presence.

We are living stones being fit together to be a resting place for the Spirit of God to dwell.

> You also, like **living stones**, are being built into a spiritual house to be a holy priesthood, offering spiritual sacrifices acceptable to God through Jesus Christ.
>
> —1 Peter 2:5

We are chosen for a divine purpose that is so much bigger than us! We have the joy of preparing ourselves as a bride for our Bridegroom!

Imagine leading worship from this posture of knowing your identity, being secure in His love, knowing you are His house, and knowing He is *for* you? As a new excitement is stirred to spend more time in His presence, and hunger is awakened to seek His Spirit to find what is in His heart to release through worship, it will change the way you prepare and lead.

Every time we lead worship, we can anticipate and expect a move of God. We can live in a heart posture of anticipation and expectancy and not be disappointed. We can long for the glory of God to come and find a home in us, because we know that He will come when we invite Him. We can live each day totally aware that we are for His glory and His glory is within us!

Picture what will happen when we dwell daily in His presence and become a spirit-led generation, living supernatural, extreme lives for *His* glory and fame?

Imagine a Church who is led by the Holy Spirit through their days and changes the atmosphere everywhere they go! When we catch hold of this and begin to live it, the face of the earth will never be the same! How the earth will rejoice when God's people remember who they are and awaken, becoming radically transformed by spending time in His presence.

What if we were convinced that today could be the day of His return and our hearts so longed for Him to come that everything else faded away? Let's respond to the call of the Lord and spend our lives in preparation for the day that Jesus returns for a bride that is pure and spotless.

We will see amazing transformation when we, the bride, live in expectancy. That level of anticipation will change the way we spend time with Him and the way we prepare and lead worship. That kind of urgency in our hearts will transform those we lead and shift the atmosphere of our churches and cities.

Prepare to lead worship with anticipation! Expect lives to be transformed and cities to explode into revival. Anticipate that the Holy Spirit will shift the atmosphere and bring a holy conviction that will cause us to prostrate ourselves in His presence for days. As each of us responds and prepares for His return, it will transform the corporate face of the bride. Our ears will be tuned to hear the words, "The Bridegroom is coming!" so we can join our voices with heaven, and in a loud voice sing:

> Worthy is the Lamb, who was slain, to receive power and wealth and wisdom and strength and honor and glory and praise!
>
> —Revelation 5:12

THREE

LOWER STILL

In Edmonton, Alberta, in 2006, I had an experience that rocked me, forever changing my heart posture in worship. I was on the stage with several amazing worship leaders from around Canada, and we were crying out for the Lord to release His glory in our nation.

At the time, I had a small grid of what that meant. I believed it would be an external event: the heavens would part, the cloud of glory would fall, and we would all be changed. In part, that could be true. But what remained to be revealed to my heart was that as we cry out for the Lord to release His glory, He responds by releasing His glory *in* us.

During one session, the presence of God was so strong that I found myself face down on the stage, weeping and travailing with all my strength. I cried out with the song that was being sung:

We lift You high and bow down low.

How high can You be?

How low can we go?

"You must Increase" by Matt Redman

As the song continued and the music moved into crescendo, I experienced my physical body needing to go lower and lower. My spirit eyes opened, and I bowed lower and lower each time we sang the line, "How low can we go?" I felt as though I had gone through the stage... then the floor... and I longed to go lower still.

I could identify with David's descriptive psalms, and if I had been writing one of my own, it would have sounded something like:

Let my body fall through the earth's very crust so You can be lifted higher and higher to the places You belong.

The heavens You created are not high enough for the glory of Your name and the fame of Your glory!

Until that time, I could not remember being so humbled by His majesty. I longed to disappear as His glory increased. Every inch of me burned with the awareness of His holiness. I knew that though I would not feel it this intensely each time I worshipped, I must worship from this low, contrite spirit so His glory will be revealed. I recognized that, as a worship leader, my job is to prepare the way for the Lord's glory, be a house for His presence, keep myself consecrated for Him, and worship from a posture of humility.

Oh, what an honor that He would trust and teach us to be in awe of *Him* as we use our gifts to prepare the way for His return.

OUR LIFE IS NOT OUR OWN

The Kingdom of God is the reverse of what the world requires. The world says to seek promotion, and the Kingdom says to go low so *Jesus* is lifted high. We must posture ourselves in humility and know that our identity is Him, and our life is not our own.

"I will send my messenger, who will prepare the way before me. Then suddenly the Lord you are seeking will come to his temple; the messenger of the covenant whom you desire, will come," says the Lord.

—Malachi 3:1

This is one of the "suddenlies" in Scripture, which finds me caught in the tension of longing for it to happen – but also gripped with holy fear that it *will* happen. We need to be a pure people, unconcerned with being seen or recognized for our gifting. The Kingdom of God is at hand and our cry must be *find a home in us, O Lord*!

COME CLOSE, LORD!

As leaders of worship, the stakes are high, and the responsibility is great. How can we lead from an overflow of our spirit if our spirit is dry? We can go through the motions and God, in His mercy, will still come. But this is called leading out of our gifting, and not out of the anointing or His glory.

When we rely on our gifting to get us through the worship set, the set itself is often very dry and void of of God's presence – a reflection of where we are at in our spirit. We can lead from this dry place but, I assure you, there is a better way.

You have probably experienced times when the busyness of life has been allowed to overtake you, and your time in His presence just didn't happen. I have led from both places – full and empty – and it is much better to be full and spill out than to be dry and feel like you are just doing a job.

It does not honor God or those you lead when you see worship as work. When leading worship becomes a grind and you have lost sight of why you do it, it might be time to step back and re-evaluate.

If you are in a desert season, don't consider yourself washed up. God is never done with us! He works in you, going into deeper places, refining you to be more like Him.

Some of the sweetest times in God's presence come when you are honest enough to admit you are dry. When your heart cries out for living water, He is faithful to come and refresh your soul. I have experienced God's refreshing while I led worship. I pour out and He pours into my spirit.

Just as there are seasons in the natural, there are also seasons in the spiritual. There are seasons of joy and celebration, weeping and sorrow, seasons of desert lands, and other times when the Lord comes closer to His people. I believe we are in an hour when the Lord is coming close, and we must respond by calling out for Him to come near.

> Two blind men were sitting by the roadside, and when they heard that Jesus was going by, they shouted, "Lord, Son of David, have mercy on us!"
>
> The crowd rebuked them and told them to be quiet, but they shouted all the louder, "Lord, Son of David, have mercy on us!"
>
> Jesus stopped and called to them, "What do you want me to do for you?" He asked.
>
> "Lord," they answered, "we want our sight."
>
> Jesus had compassion on them and touched their eyes. Immediately they received their sight and followed Him.
>
> —Matthew 20:31-34

As the bride, we have been calling because we long for Him to come close. Many songs we write and sing are around this very topic. Many worship leaders have heard the voice of the Lord in this season, and in their radical pursuit of His presence, they shout all the louder in desperation.

Now it's happening – He is turning to look at us and ask, "What do you want Me to do for you?" But do we even know how to answer this question?

Yes, we want our eyes opened. We want to make Him first so that our worship is an overflow of our full spirits. We desire our worship to touch His heart and draw and attract His presence. But, practically, what does this look like? How do we go low so He can be lifted high? How do we draw and attract Him? How do we take these concepts from theory to reality and make them practical for our lives? How do we begin to answer His question, "What do you want me to do for you?"

OUR SOURCE

One of the most pivotal actions we can take is to carve out time for Him in our daily life. Worship and prayer need to become like oxygen to us.

I have a good friend, Tracey, who says it like this: Imagine if we were to take a big gulp of air first thing in the morning and say, "Ok, this better get me through the day as I am really swamped and simply don't have time to breathe!"

What a ridiculous concept! Yet, this is often what we do in the spirit realm. We put worshipping our Maker last on our to-do list, along with reading His Word, talking with Him, and making Him part of everything we do.

Just like the Kingdom of God works in an upside-down, inside-out way, it is the same with carving out time for Jesus. As you make Him a priority and fit your life around *Him*, He becomes your source. You become homesick for His presence. When you have been too long away, your physical body begins to pull toward the need to be alone with Him. You identify with the Scriptures that say:

> You are my refuge and my shield. I have put my hope in your word.
>
> —Psalm 119:114

> If you belonged to the world it would love you as its own. As it is, you do not belong to the world, but I have chosen you out of the world. That is why the world hates you.
>
> —John 15:19

As you spend time with Him, your perspective shifts, and you realize that, while your feet walk the earth, heaven is your home. You become a stranger in a strange land. The more heavenly minded you are, the more earthly good you are! As you are in continual relationship with the Father, He shares His heart with you so that you can be His extension on this earth. The more you know Him, the more you will impact your world.

I have many responsibilities. Life is full, and when my lamp is empty, it can be hard to get through my day; they become long, arduous, and fleshly. With life being so full, I must rise early, and seek Him when the house is quiet. I look forward to getting up before the sun to spend time with Jesus. He centers me, and as His beautiful presence surrounds and fills me, my head is immediately lifted.

My time with Him gives me energy to jump into the day, and, yet, it is so much more than that! I have energy but I don't want to leave His presence. I am so hungry for more of Jesus that I look for any opportunity to be alone with Him. The more I pursue Him, the more He pursues me. He becomes my first love, and I want to be one who diligently seeks Him. I want to daily stand before Him and say, "You are my everything. I lift You high and bow down low; how high can You be, and how low can I go?"

FOUR

SATURATED SOUND

I was born a leader. I had a competitive streak that made me want to be number one, regardless of what it did to others. My mom talks about me, at the age of three in the church nursery, lining up all the other two and three year-olds on the riding toys and leading a parade around the room.

At the age of eight, I volunteered to lead worship in our weekly chapels at school. I constantly told the other kids what to do and how to do it. I organized everyone around me. I would make up games, and change the rules on the fly as soon as I started to lose.

I always innately knew my authority and often used it – and others – to get what I wanted. While at times I led for selfish reasons, as I matured in God's presence and my mentors spoke into my life, I began to realize I could not accomplish what was in my heart on my own.

We each carry a unique sound in the spirit, and we need each other for the fullness of heaven's sound to be released. We cannot get there alone; God designed us to be joined together.

Often, worship leaders are visionaries – we see heaven's agenda and where the Lord wants to take the corporate body through worship. What we sometimes overlook in this process is the value of a team working together toward the goals that are in our hearts collectively.

The story of Paul and Silas in prison is a great example of worshipping and standing in Christ's authority as a team. They encouraged one another and joined their voices together to sing spiritual songs and hymns. As a result, they shifted the atmosphere (see Ephesians 5:19).

Around midnight Paul and Silas were praying and singing hymns to God, and the other prisoners were listening. Suddenly, there was a massive earthquake, and the prison was shaken to its foundations. All the doors immediately flew open, and **the chains of every prisoner fell off!**

—Acts 16:25-26, NLT

As worship leaders, this story speaks to who we are called to be. No matter the season of the soul (in this case, severely beaten and flogged), Paul and Silas were found faithful before the Lord with their lamps full. Before the Lord, they fanned their inner flame (see 2 Timothy 1:6-7) and began to praise, not because they felt like it, but because God was worthy.

I believe they led others into the posture of worship as they simply sang out His praise. They shifted the prison, both literally and figuratively, that held others captive. By faith, they took hold of the truth of Jesus, proclaimed it with their mouths, and believed with all their hearts that worthy was the Lamb to receive all honor, glory, power, and strength.

Like Paul and Silas, we hold the power and the authority to shift atmospheres in the spirit and in the natural. As born again, spirit-filled believers of Jesus, we can declare through our songs, believe with our hearts, and watch with our eyes the transformative presence of God shake us to our foundations.

When we sing from the posture of faith and anticipation and believe that anything is possible, we will see the doors of prisons fly open and chains fall off of God's precious people.

THE ENCOUNTER

(June, 2009, journal entry)

I was in worship Tuesday morning, and the fear and presence of the Lord came over me in a very significant way. I felt the Lord begin to speak very clearly, and I believe that what He spoke was for worship leaders.

I felt Him say that I am not allowed to waste my time in worship anymore. I am not allowed to meander through worship until I feel satisfied or until I have an experience. He impressed on me to *immediately* shift the way I approach and lead worship.

He revealed that we each hold the potential to shift atmospheres through worship. You have the potential because He did it first. When you know your authority and who you are in Him, His spirit will resonate on each note that you sing, play, or dance. Each sound you release will be a deathblow to the enemy.

Every blow that the Lord lays down will be to the sound of the tambourine and harp.

—Isaiah 30:30

He trains my hands for war, and my fingers for battle.

—Psalm 144:1

This is the year of the favor of the Lord, this is the day of the vengeance of our God to comfort all who mourn ... and provide for those who grieve in Zion – to bestow on them a crown of beauty instead of ashes, the oil of gladness instead of mourning, and a garment of praise instead of a spirit of despair. They will be called oaks of righteousness, a planting of the LORD for the display of his splendor.

—Isaiah 61:2-3

WASTING TIME IN WORSHIP

When the Lord spoke to me that I had wasted time in my worship, I was instantly undone and repentant. What did that mean? How had I wasted time?

Mostly, it had to do with the way I approached leading a worship set. My heart posture was very demeaning toward those I led. I would anticipate that it was going to take several songs before the congregation was awake enough – naturally and spiritually –

to really worship. I had a pompous, stuck-up attitude that said I, as their amazing leader, was prepared in my spirit, but they were not ready to worship.

I was arrogant and self-centered. With just one phrase, the Lord revealed the blackness inside my heart. As I repented before Him, He washed me clean with His precious blood and gave me another chance.

The Holy Spirit also impressed on me another area of sin. As I led worship, I would meander through the set list, unmotivated to seek Him until I had an experience in His presence. It was only when I began to experience His presence that I felt motivated to find more. It was only then that I began to anticipate He could actually do something during worship. It was so selfish, and it needed to end!

Time is short – we live in the last days. We are in a season where every second counts. By His grace alone we can accomplish everything He asks of us. The Lord called me to shift my approach immediately. I can say that from that day on, my heart has been in a different posture.

He then began to reveal the potential authority each worship leader and team member carries. When we are postured in faith and expectancy, we can speak to the wind and waves, and they will be still.

This is the posture we are to continuously walk in, not just for ourselves but also for those who can't do it themselves. We are called to bridge the gap between heaven and earth, between the Father's heart and His children.

CLEAR CHANNELS

Holy Spirit next showed me a vision of a soundboard. Each channel was connected directly to God so that we could project His notes, sounds, and songs with clarity. As He inhabited each sound, we became supernatural carriers of His glory and presence – He chooses to use us to fulfill His dreams and purposes.

Be a clear channel: so connected to God that everywhere you lead worship is filled with the sound of faith. Sing and believe what you are singing! When you produce fruit and have victories in your personal worship, you will do the same in the public arena.

PULL DOWN GIANTS

Ask the Lord to thoroughly saturate each note that you sing to release His authority and presence. Sing with faith! Just as faithless prayers do not accomplish much in the spirit, faithless songs can also be counter-productive.

Our authority is for pulling down "Goliaths." This can also be done on behalf of those within the Kingdom who are too afraid. It cannot be done alone, so camaraderie is more important now than ever before.

The foundation of our worship is *Kingdom*. I remember Ray Hughes talking about perspective. He said that the Israelites saw Goliath and were intimidated by the giant, but David saw Goliath and saw a target he couldn't miss!

When our perspective is from a Kingdom viewpoint, we understand that God has delivered the giants into our hands because of who HE is in us! We can stand, like David, without fear in the face of Goliath, because we know we *are His sounds*, released to hit the mark and conquer the enemy.

Seek and encounter the Lord in your secret place of worship. As you do so, He will direct your path and search your heart. He wants every part of you. He longs for you to live in the fullness of your potential, wholeheartedly His and undivided in your affection and attention.

God created you in His image, and with Him, all things are possible. Partner with Father God, Jesus, the Holy Spirit, and with those in your life whose hearts beat hard after Him.

Five

HIDDEN

Our highest goal is to bring honor to God. When we place Him first and highest, everything else comes into order. A motto I choose to live by is: I am a part of a nameless, faceless generation that does not care if our name is remembered. I want those I encounter to remember that the glory of God was there, His presence came, and He was magnified.

In our effort to get out of the way and let it be Jesus who is seen, it is important to note that this does not mean to disconnect from those you are ministering to. Relationship is so important, and connecting with the congregation, either through personal stories, comments, or exhortation is all part of being a good worship leader.

Allow the life and light on the inside of you to spill out and infuse the congregation with joy, faith, hope and anticipation. Share your heart from the place of being hidden under the shadow of His wings. This allows it to be Jesus who is seen.

In Psalms there are many references to the "shadow of His wings." The concept of being hidden was one David was very familiar with. He knew how to hide himself in the Lord, and he often wrote about God as his refuge, and His glorious presence as the one thing he would diligently seek after.

> Keep me as the apple of your eye; hide me in the shadow of your wings.
>
> —Psalm 17:8

> How priceless is your unfailing love, O God! People take refuge in the **shadow** of your wings.
>
> —Psalm 36:7

> Because you are my help, I sing in the **shadow** of your wings.
>
> —Psalm 63:7

> Whoever dwells in the shelter of the Most High will rest in the **shadow** of the Almighty.
>
> —Psalm 91:1

To remain hidden in the Lord is not an excuse to hide behind insecurities, fears, or religion. It is to place yourself under the total authority of Jesus Christ; to be motivated by and for Him, and to decrease in your earthly desires so that He can increase.

Our goal is to have the unclean portions of our lives disappear, and be filled with righteousness and purity so that Jesus is seen in every area of our lives. Being hidden does not mean to stop being who you are. We are the most alive when we live out the truth of who we are created to be and what we are purposed to do. Is this goal achievable in this lifetime?

> Jesus looked at them and said, "With man this is impossible, but not with God; **all things** are **possible** with God."
>
> —Mark 10:27

God's word is truth, and He says we are victorious! We must never give up pursuing Him, because it is in *Him* that everything is available to us. It *is* possible to come into all that has Jesus for us! We can be those who stand for righteousness in the darkness and who shine the pure light of love through our lives of worship.

BRIDGES

Many years ago, I did a prophetic act with a phenomenal group of worshippers at the Church of Zion in Vancouver, BC. Mei Chu (one of my worship mentors) was preparing with the team to lead the worship service. We earnestly cried out to the Lord to hide us, let Him and His glory be seen, and let us be pure, clean vessels for Him to work through.

The Lord instructed us to set up our instruments along the front row and leave the stage bare. It physically represented what we carried in our spirits. The result of being obedient was abandoned worship before the Lord: not looking to the right or the left, but straight into His face. It was God-centered, God-directed worship.

The congregation responded to the call of God and worshipped with complete freedom, totally focused on the real worship Leader, the Holy Spirit. That morning was a beautiful reminder from the Lord of who we are and what we are called to do.

We live within the tension of getting out of God's way and being God's voice to the people. Do I believe that we should lead worship from the front row all the time? Not at all! There is something very precious about being able to relate to those you lead in worship.

Bruce Friesen, senior pastor of my home church, Lion of Judah Ministries, in Victoria, BC, shared a beautiful picture of our position as worship leaders: We are to keep our ear to the chest of the Father, our finger on the pulse of the people, and bridge the two.

When you read a Scripture, share an encounter, revelation, dream, or just ask the people how they are, it is important because it builds the sense of community in a corporate worship service. We are called to be like Jesus through our words and deeds, and He built relationships with those He was called to serve. He would talk to the people, tell stories, and relate what He said to their lives and cultural situations.

Again, you can't live so "hidden" that you become an island. It will make the congregation uncomfortable to go into the deep places of worship with you. Why would you follow someone that you don't know or trust to a place you have never been before?

When you share your heart and allow yourself to become vulnerable and transparent, it is so much easier to worship together with a common goal. Relationship is foundational to doing anything together in the Kingdom of God. Why would it be any different when leading worship?

Getting out of God's way and being hidden in Him does not mean that we are so "spiritual" and impersonal that we do not relate to those around us — just the contrary! While we are not to be *of* the world, we *are* called to be *in* it. Getting out of God's way and being hidden is a heart posture. Our hearts are submitted to Him, and our minds are set on Him, but we still need to be relatable to the ones God has called us to have influence with.

Obedience to the call of God means that you live bridging heaven and earth, while being authentically you, and being God's glory. Being authentic is not easy in any stream, but it can be especially difficult for those called to the area of the arts and worship. It is difficult to filter out the many influences and find who you really are and what sound you carry.

FIND YOUR SOUND

We all carry the DNA of our Father, and His sound is unique in each of us. Your natural tone, musical style, and sound may be the product of environment and other influences, but your spiritual sound is all yours.

How do you discover this sound? It's discovered by spending time alone with Jesus. When you foster an intimate relationship with Him, He reveals who you are and what sound He has given you to carry in the spirit. It is through intimacy with Him that your heart is unveiled and your true sound is discovered.

Our sound is in the spirit; it is how we commune with the Lord, and it is how we worship in spirit and in truth (John 4 23-24). It can translate into the natural as well, but is mostly released through our spirit as we worship.

People carry many sounds and many sound combinations. Some examples of the sounds, as I define them, are:

+ intimacy
+ celebration
+ warfare
+ justice
+ intercession
+ declaration
+ prophecy

As you read the list, it is possible that one or more words seemed to jumped off the page at you. This could be one of the sounds that define you.

RELEASE YOUR SOUND

My primary sound tends to be a mixture of intercession, prophecy, and declaration. When I lead worship and allow the Holy Spirit to flow through my voice, I release my sound through the songs I sing. For example, I can sing any song about His goodness, and I will begin to naturally flow into declaring Scripture about His goodness. This releases hope into the atmosphere through declaration of His Word.

I then begin to prophesy that He is good in the midst of the specific circumstances I am "picking up" in the congregation. This will lead me naturally into a song of intercession over those who do not believe God is good.

My song of intercession will flow back into the original song that we were singing, completing the prophetic worship circle. God is released most when I allow the sound He placed inside me to naturally influence the songs I sing.

SONG SELECTION

Practically, there is also something you can do with song selection, according to the context of the service you are leading. So often, we choose songs because we like them; we have them in our current rotation, and we randomly looked through our repertoire and they looked like a good choice. They're not chosen because they're actually going to be the right songs for the service or conference.

Leading worship always presents a great opportunity for you to seek the Lord and ask what it is on His heart that He wants you to release. This is a humbling responsibility. Just because a song has opened doors in the spirit realm before, or you experience God's presence when you hear it on the CD, is not a good enough reasons to choose it.

For example, singing a very wordy, deep, prophetic song in a gathering of many different denominations, with people at many different places on their worship journey, may serve to simply devalue the original gift of that song. As a result, you will find very little spiritual weight on the song as you release it.

There are some songs that are released from heaven as mandate songs. They are released in specific moments, times, and places in order to shift things in both the spirit and the natural. When you randomly throw one of these songs into a set list, you can actually minimize the original heart and burden within that song. Always evaluate where you are and whom you are leading. Then, prayerfully, choose songs accordingly.

JOY-FILLED WORSHIP

It is important to note that there is unspeakable joy in His presence! Sometimes, as prophetic worship leaders, we can get stuck in such a serious posture. His

JOY comes in the morning... allow it to overtake you! It will open your heart and the hearts of those around you! Let His joy fill you and guide your worship.

> The Lord your God is with you, the Mighty Warrior who saves. He will take great delight in you; in his love he will no longer rebuke you, but will rejoice over you with singing.
>
> —Zephaniah 3:17

Remain hidden in Him, and remain intimate with Him. Keep your head on His chest, and use His heartbeat as your guide while keeping your finger on the pulse of those the Lord has called you to lead.

Six

THE DEEP

The way to personal intimacy with the Father is to discover your keys of intimacy: the keys that unlock your heart and allow direct access to Him. Just as there are many different people, there are many keys of intimacy. Some may feel closest to the Father when they research facts, study science, scripture, or history, etc. Others may find they experience the presence of God most when they are in nature or that their heart is unlocked through the arts.

I have found that my main key of intimacy is when I sing. The more I let my heart be unlocked in intimate times with Jesus, the more my destiny became clear. I have learned that I experience God's presence and pleasure the most when I release my heart before Him in song – I sing from my heart, not out of what I *think* He would like to hear.

This was very important for me to learn. I realized that I get in the way of the prophetic flow when I sing what I think will make God love and value me more, or will make me more holy and righteous. This was often how I approached God, even when I was alone and singing to Him. I had to learn to let go and not worry about what I thought might make me look the best. I had to learn how to minister to God, not *perform* for Him.

I minister to the Lord when I take off my mask and become real and vulnerable in His presence. I have learned to trust Him with the secrets in my heart. I now spend time singing *to* Him, singing *with* Him, and listening to Him sing over me. I have learned to engage my heart, let go of my rationale, and simply rest in His presence. If you do not know this intimacy or this experience, ask. Ask the Father to help you let go and simply *be*.

INTIMACY LEADS TO DESTINY

We can see the connection between intimacy and destiny in the natural realm where intimacy is designed to result in pregnancy. It is the same in the spiritual realm. Through intimacy you become pregnant with dreams, desires, and destiny, which grow and develop as you spend more time with the Lord.

As you nurture and cultivate the dreams and destiny He reveals to you, His favor and pleasure increases. You also realize that they are not *your* dreams, desires, and destiny, but they are *His* dreams for you, *His* desires for you, and *His* destiny for you. When you come to this realization, it gives you the strength and courage to do anything, because you know He is *for* you, He loves you, and His strength is your strength.

CULTIVATED DESTINY

You may not know it, but the journey to discover your dreams, desires, and destiny may be well underway. As a child, I was cultivated to be who He created me to be. It is not until I look back and reflect that I realize He was after me then just as much as He is now!

As a young girl, one of my favorite things was to sit at the piano and play all the songs in the praise and worship book from my church. I had so much fun figuring out the chords and singing along – I had no idea I was training myself to play by ear. My heart was so alive as I would get lost in the music! I didn't fully understand that I was worshipping, but I knew God was happy with me. I remember often feeling how proud He was of me. Being an egocentric child, I was convinced it was because my voice and playing were awesome. But it wouldn't have made a bit of difference if I couldn't sing a note on pitch – He was after my heart!

The truth is that I loved my own voice. Once, while performing at a church-camp at the age of four, I shoved my partner out of the way (who started crying, poor guy), grabbed the microphone, went to the front of the stage, and sang with everything I had! I loved singing into the microphone and being in the front. I loved my voice so much that I would sing for hours onto blank tapes and then play back my songs just so I could amaze myself with my talent.

It's hilarious, but it's also part of who God made me to be: a voice in His Kingdom. He had to deal with the posture of my heart – wanting to be seen and wanting people's praise – but the basic destiny was always there.

When I recorded onto the tapes, I would open my Bible and sing the Psalms. I thought they were beautiful and made great song lyrics. My motivation wasn't worship; it was to hear myself on tape. However, a heart of worship was cultivated as I declared and sang the scriptures.

The presence of God was very real to me in those times. My motivation began to shift from my desire to hear myself to a desire to be with Jesus. I did not have the language to describe what I was experiencing, but I began to crave those precious times with Him. God's glory and presence were with me, and I was being myself, enjoying the gift He gave to me to enjoy – my musicality.

Honestly, it could have gone either way for me as a child. I could have very easily gone down the path of self-promotion. I wanted people to hear, notice, and be pleased with me. I wanted recognition to feed the place in me that desired to be accepted and to be the star.

Mercifully, God revealed Himself to my heart and began to heal the places that needed affirmation for what I could do, rather than for who I was. As He healed me, the need to be the star decreased, and the need to promote Him became a priority. It was a subtle transformation that happened over time. God taught me that He was my biggest fan.

THE CALL TO DEEPER

In my continual discovery of who I am in Him, one of the most pivotal moments happened during prayer and worship one morning. I was reading in Luke, and I began to meditate on one simple phrase that the Holy Spirit highlighted to me: *Put out into deep waters* (Luke 5:4).

I consecrated my imagination to the Lord, and He took me into a vision of a whirlpool. I was aware that I was looking at the deepest part of the ocean; there was no land on any horizon. I was drawn toward the swirling water, and I was terrified as I looked into the abyss, but I was aware that this was actually happening on the inside of my spirit. God was stirring the deepest part of me. He led me to Psalm 42:7 that says, "Deep calls unto deep."

I was taken into another part of the vision and saw myself in a boat with Jesus. We were traveling into the ocean, again to the deepest part. He asked me what I wanted to do, and I replied, "Oh, I'm cool. I'll just stay in the boat. Thanks for asking!" My heart was beating hard, and I was afraid of what would come next.

He asked me if I wanted to swim. (Now, in the natural, I love swimming. I grew up on the West Coast of British Columbia, Canada, surrounded by oceans, rivers, and lakes. I was an avid swimmer, spending every spare second of my summers in the water.) I replied, "NO, THANKS! I'm good... *I don't know what's down there.*"

As soon as the words were out of my mouth, I felt the heat of His conviction sweetly begin to burn me. I became undone in His presence as He began to reveal my heart and how fearful I was of what I couldn't see and control. He again led me to read Luke, followed by Daniel.

> Put out into deep water.
>
> —Luke 5:4

> He reveals deep and hidden things; He knows what lies in darkness and light dwells within Him.
>
> —Daniel 2:22

The Holy Spirit reminded me of a word that a dear friend, Wanda Fost, had spoken over me a few years prior. She said that I was made to go into the dark and hidden places to find the treasure. The Lord finished my encounter in His presence by sealing into my heart: *You were made for the deep.*

Let it also be sealed in *your* heart – you were made for the deep! You were made to experience an intimate relationship with God as Father and Friend. You were created to minister to Him and to be ministered to by Him. You have a destiny, and He will continue to unlock you in His presence. His word is true, and His promises are yes and amen (2 Corinthians 1:20).

> For the Lord your God is living among you. He is a mighty savior. He will take delight in you with gladness. With his love, he will calm all your fears. He will rejoice over you with joyful songs.
>
> —Zephaniah 3:17, NLT

SEVEN

INDUSTRY

I n this hour, there are some areas in which the line between godlessness and holiness can be unclear. Major social and justice issues are so normalized in our society that, unless we go back to scripture, we can become confused as to where God calls us to stand. Worship is one area that often becomes watered down and lukewarm. Unless we go back to scripture, it is very easy to buy into the cultural and social standards that define worship.

INDUSTRY   73

WE NEED MORE THAN TALENT

In my experience of church culture, worship often becomes the responsibility of musicians who are capable. This may *sound* like a good plan, but just because someone is a musician doesn't mean the Lord has appointed him or her to the *office* of leading worship. We have watered down the requirements of who can be on the worship team to natural talents, and, as a result, the presence of God has also been diluted.

This is scary business. When we step on the stage, we step into the position of the head of the army (see 2 Chronicles 13:12; 20:21). When someone who does not carry the mandate, authority, or understanding of what it means to lead in Spirit and truth is released to lead worship, they and their family may be needlessly exposed to attacks from the enemy's camp. God has given them the gift of music, but if they do not understand the responsibility of leadership, there will be a concert performance instead of worship.

Some time ago, I was driving home from a conference in Vancouver, BC, when I was taken into an open vision. In the vision I saw a temple, much as we see depicted in period movies from ancient Roman civilization. Inside the temple were tables covered with CDs, DVDs, books, manuals, and other products. I became aware that they were all worship products.

My vision continued, and Jesus came into the temple. He became angry and, gripped with a holy violence, began flipping the tables over. I watched Him clear the room and all of a sudden, like a gigantic neon sign, the word "INDUSTRY" flashed through my spirit. I physically felt His grief and anger that worship had become an industry.

Worship was designed as a pure expression of our love – a place of communion between heaven and earth, between God and man. It caused the Lord pain that it was being used for unrighteous gain and not the way it was designed: for His honor and glory. Sometimes the people of God can choose compromising situations and our pride and carnality can sway our motivation for worship.

INTERCESSION & MERCY

I was pulled into intercession and prayed that we, as His worshippers, would remember whom we are and why we have been given our talents. I cried out for His mercy to invade the hearts of individuals who had been deceived and sideswiped.

It is important to note that we are all called to different positions within God's Kingdom. I strongly believe some Christian artists are called to the marketplace to work in the music industry and shine the light of Jesus through everything they do.

It is impossible for us to judge the hearts of man. That is God's job. It is crucial that we believe the best of people, and pray that God will raise up Christians who will live for Him in the music industry. We must not step into judgment, or feel more holy and pure because we worship in the church. We must stand on guard for our brothers and sisters who are taking ground in the industry; who are being light and salt and taking a stand for righteousness and purity! We must cover these precious ones in prayer and believe that God's glory will be seen through their music and their lives.

It is important to remember that we cannot see into each other's hearts. Just because someone holds a "worship leader" title does not guarantee they understand and live the truths of worship – just as a CD can be labeled "worship" but may be motivated by something different. Ultimately, we are only responsible before the Lord for the choices that *we* make; so choose to live in holiness.

RELEASE CONTROL

Whenever you have a stage and a microphone, you have power and a choice. You have the choice to get out of the way and make room for the power of the Holy

Spirit, or you make the choice to control and manipulate with *your* power.

The spirit of control is rooted in fear. We fear what we don't understand and then we try to control it. We fear what we can't see so we try to manipulate situations to protect ourselves. When we lead worship with a spirit of control, we attempt to control the Holy Spirit and emotionally manipulate the people, whether or not we understand that's what we are doing.

One time as I led worship, I was singing to the Lord that He is in control; He is the leader, we are following hard after Him, and we are fully His. In my heart and mind, I was totally sincere. However, there was another layer within my heart that the Lord needed to strip off.

He took me into a vision where He gently challenged me to lock eyes with Him. That alone would have been enough of a healing experience for me! To lock eyes with someone is a vulnerable exercise and one that was extremely uncomfortable for me. But I took the risk and locked eyes with Him – I felt healing through His gaze, and I became undone. In that moment, I felt my body being pulled toward Him, and what I experienced next terrified me.

Through His eyes, I entered into Jesus and began to free-fall inside of Him. Instantly, I panicked because I had lost control! I had nothing to hold onto and nothing to hold me back. I was aware that He is endless, and I would be able to fall forever into the depths of who He is. I heard Him ask, "How far do you want to go?" His voice was peace, but my mind would not release me to enjoy Him and see where it was He wanted me to go.

I fought the vision and came out of it totally aware that Jesus was asking me to deal with the issues of control and fear. I immediately postured myself in repentance. I asked for His mercy and forgiveness to flood my soul where I was afraid to let Him have total control. His love and peace immediately met me, and I knew that in the spirit realm it was done. Now I had to walk it out in the earthly realm.

Until that experience, I didn't realize just how much control I was still holding onto when I worshipped. I was controlling how much I gave to Him and how much I would receive from Him. I saw how much I feared to fully allow Him to lead *me* as I led the people. I was still afraid of making mistakes and of being unlovable.

As I reflected on this experience, I began to receive His healing love into my heart. The Holy Spirit reassured me that I am completely loved and totally okay. I do not have to perform for Him or for those He has given me the privilege of leading. God wanted me to trust Him and learn to take risks so He can lead me into the unknown places to find treasure.

It is time for the Levites, the ones chosen to lead the corporate bride in worship, to rise! It is time to let go of fear, control, selfish ambition, and gain. Now is the time to discover all God has created us to be as worshippers, and go lower still so that He is exalted to His rightful place.

Ask the Lord to guard your heart and mind against all that would try to pull you away from His purpose for your life, especially in the area of ministry through worship. He is faithful to listen and pursue us. Be thankful! Give up control so that God can kill the rock star inside of you and purify your sound, making you wholly His.

Whether you are called to minister in the church or in the marketplace, purpose in your heart to remain pure and holy so that your gifts can be used to exalt Jesus in the nations. Determine that *He* will be your source and focus, and live to reflect *Him*!

EIGHT

THE JOURNEY

In every worship setting, there are worshippers in many different stages of their journey. Typically, there are those who understand how to contend in worship, how to enter into the deep places quickly, and how to seek the Lord with abandonment. There are those learning to worship and exploring new freedoms, and still others who stand with blank looks on their faces, hands in their pockets, seemingly disengaged.

The mature worship leader can look at the different stages and not be bothered that there is not one hundred percent outward engagement. They know how to love the people where they are and don't worry about the exterior. Their focus is on bridging the Kingdom of Heaven to earth.

When you are still growing in maturity, the thought patterns tend to be much different. These are some extreme and exaggerated examples to give you an idea of what placing value in external expression looks like:

+ What's wrong with these people? Don't they know we are WORSHIPPING? What are they thinking?

+ They are wasting my time AND God's time. They might as well go home, it would make my job easier.

+ Good thing it isn't about them. This is for the GLORY of GOD.

+ I am going straight into the intimate place of worship, and I don't really care if they come with me or not!

Here are extreme and exaggerated examples of self-righteous and judgmental thoughts:

+ Wow, look at the way these people are responding to MY worship.

- I am an amazing leader. I would say ninety percent of this congregation is engaged.

- God is so right to have chosen me as a leader.

- I have played a major part in allowing these people to experience the presence of God. Because of the way I am leading, they will never be the same.

- If someone else led today, there would have been nothing for these people.

- Thank You, Jesus, that I am Your vessel of worship, because without my talents, You couldn't have been glorified.

Sound at *all* familiar? If I am being honest, I have thought something along these lines at one point or another. Wow! How self-righteous we can be to think we know better than someone else or have allowed someone the privilege of experiencing true worship.

When we think that we have it figured out and can read someone's heart, based on their expression during worship, we are walking in dangerous territory. No one, except God, can read another's heart. It is so important to not step into judgment of another person. We must stay in a posture of love, mercy, and grace toward one another.

GRACE & LOVE

The Lord gave Lorraine Frisen, one of our senior leaders, a beautiful picture about the different stages of our journey as the Body of Christ.

She saw the Israelite masses as they crossed the Red Sea – millions of people, all moving forward. Some were already on the other side of the sea, rejoicing, and some were in the middle of the ocean, trembling and unable to see if there was an end in sight. Others were just entering the waters, and some were not even aware they were heading toward the ocean. Everyone was in a different stage of the journey, but everyone was moving forward. Those who had already made it through the waters had to keep moving forward to make room for those coming out behind them.

The point is very simple: Grace and love for one another need to abound in the body of Christ.

OUR ROLE

Typically, those called to minister through worship are called to be in the front of the army.

After consulting the people, Jehoshaphat appointed men to sing to the LORD and to praise him for the splendor of his holiness as they went out at the head of the army, saying:

"Give thanks to the LORD, for his love endures forever."

—2 Chronicles 20:21

Our God-ordained position is not something to boast or become proud about, it is simply our role in the body. Our job is to see where Jesus is going, and listen as He turns and says, "Come over here, it is *so* much better." We follow Him and then turn to those following *us* and say, "Come over here it is *so* much better.

In no way can we *ever* afford to feel superior or judgmental toward those who are just beginning their journey into the sea. In fact, we need to send the message, "Keep coming forward. It is *so* much better over here!"

The Lord explained my role as a worship leader like this: I am one of the first into the river, and I am one of the last out. I hang out in the water and encourage others to come in, staying there until everyone has experienced the river's flow. Sometimes I lend a hand to those who are not sure what to do once they are in the water. I encourage those who are enjoying the experience in the river, while always calling to those on the shore to "Come in here, it is *so* much better once you are in!"

PASTORAL & PROPHETIC

So, how do we value where people are and still follow the Spirit of God? We walk in the tension of both the pastoral and the prophetic.

In *extreme pastoral* leading, you would create your worship set based on the people's needs, making sure everyone will be comfortable with the song choices and direction of the worship. You tailor the set to the pastor's direction and the people's preference.

In *extreme prophetic* leading, you would think about what you would like to see happen in the set – you're going to go where God is going, regardless of whether the people can follow or not. They do not matter. What matters is where you know in your heart to go.

In a more balanced approach, you seek the Lord's heart for what He wants to release. You create your set based on where the people are currently able to engage in worship, but you seek to stretch them beyond what they have known, all the while remembering that you will not leave them behind. You will push in and then come back to round up those you lost. Then you will push in a little farther and, again, come back to gather those who couldn't follow.

This balance is accomplished by using familiar, accessible songs to gather and focus as a congregation; stepping into some prophetic or spontaneous songs which follow the Spirit; making declarations and then coming back with something familiar and worshipful to refocus and reengage *all* of the people.

Don Potter is an amazing example of leading worship in the tension of the pastoral and the prophetic. He is one of the best I have experienced. I strongly encourage you to get his resources and learn from one of the fathers of worship in this generation.[1]

HONOR AUTHORITY

Living in the tension of the pastoral and prophetic requires learning how to honor those who are in authority over you, such as pastors and senior leaders. God has given the authority and ownership over the growth, care, and development of your local church to one or more pastors. As a worship leader, especially one with a prophetic bend, you will often feel you know where to go and how to get there. It is critical that you learn humility, love, and honor toward your leadership. Do not be a leader who, out of arrogance, leads in the direction *you* want to go, regardless of where your

---

[1] You can find Don Potter's products at www.potterhausmusic.com.

pastors have asked you to go. This is displeasing to God and in direct defiance of what He has said:

> Humble yourselves, therefore, under God's mighty hand, that He may lift you up in due time.
>
> —1 Peter 5:6

As difficult as it can be to have limitations placed on you in a corporate setting, when you know how to worship in a deep and true way, honor your leaders – honor what they ask. You do not have to agree with it, but make sure you keep your spirit in a position of honor. It is not hypocritical to do what they have asked when you don't feel it is right. Keep focused and know it is *all* worship, including your honor.

Yes, there may be a better way or a deeper way. Yes, there is more freedom than we can imagine in Christ, but remember the picture of the Red Sea. You may be farther into the ocean but turn around and keep bidding others to come: "You can do it, don't give up. It is *so* much better over here."

Ask the Lord for opportunities to worship outside of your local congregation. Put together a group of worshippers who long to explore the deep places. Get worship resources that will challenge and inspire you. Worship like your heart desires on your own at home.

Keep your heart and hands pure in the process, and God will be honored.

You will find that if you value relationship with those in authority over you, trust will develop. As trust develops, the Lord will give you windows of opportunity to share your perspective and your heart. Trust that God desires the best for your leader and that He is after their heart. As much as you desire to see your leaders and church community walking in true freedom, God wants it even *more*.

Above all, keep your spirit pure. If it is simply too much and the battle seems too tough, ask the Lord to reveal His strategies for you. Ask trusted friends to seek the Lord with you for answers. You might be surprised by what the Lord will say.

As you learn to walk in love and grace toward your local community and really believe that you are not higher, more educated, or enlightened than everyone else around you, and as you understand that we are all on a journey moving forward together, your heart will grow and expand with love for the body of Christ.

When it comes right down to it, the heart of worship we are called to carry is very simple: It is all about Christ. We are not rock stars seeking a stage, or our name in lights. We are humble servants who seek to go low and lift Him high.

Come, let us sing for joy to the Lord; let us shout aloud to the Rock of our salvation.

Let us come before him with thanksgiving and extol him with music and song.

For the Lord is the great God, the great King above all gods.

In his hand are the depths of the earth, and the mountain peaks belong to him.

The sea is his, for he made it, and his hands formed the dry land.

Come, let us bow down in worship, let us kneel before the Lord our Maker;

For he is our God and we are the people of his pasture, the flock under his care.

—Psalm 95:1-7

Be whom you are called and created to be! Reflect our great God through your life, your heart, and your music. Release the sound God has placed on the inside of you; stand amazed as His presence invades everything you put your hand to and every note that comes out of your mouth as you worship. *Expect great things!*

Great is the LORD and most worthy of praise; his greatness no one can fathom.

—Psalm 145:3

THE AUTHOR

Sandy Lockhart leads worship infused with a passion to see God honored and glorified and His presence released. She longs to see an army of God's people arise, who are fully awake and alive, to release lasting revival throughout the earth. Sandy brings a prophetic unlocking into the atmosphere, which allows the Church to remember their identity as sons and daughters of the King. She desires that each believer would be fully His, encounter the living God, be set ablaze by love and joy, and change the world around them.

Sandy has participated in several albums, including her newest solo release, *Where I Belong*. Currently, Sandy lives in Victoria, BC, Canada, with her husband Tim and their children Isaac, Jonvie, Eden, and David.

To request Sandy for your event or to purchase her product please contact:

unlockedministries@gmail.com.

Additional copies of this book and
other book titles from XP Publishing
are available at: XPministries.com

BULK ORDERS:
We have bulk/wholesale prices for
stores and ministries.
Please contact:
usaresource@xpministries.com
and the resource manager will help you.
Our books are also available to
bookstores through
Anchordistributors.com
For Canadian bulk orders, please contact:
resource@xpministries.com